D0390179

Employee Engagement

Lessons from the Mouse House!

Pete Blank

No part of this book may be reproduced in any form or by any electronic or mechanical means including, but not limited to, printing, photocopying, audio or video recording, electronic replication, information storage and retrieval systems, and internet distribution without permission in writing from the author. The only exception is by a reviewer, who may quote short excerpts in a review. All international copyright laws apply.

All trademarks, service marks, product names and company names are assumed to be the property of their respective owners, and are used only for reference. There is no implied endorsement by those entities. Likewise, the fact that an organization or website is referenced in this work as a potential source of further information does not mean that author or the publisher endorses, has confirmed, or warrants the information provided in this book or in those references.

Visit us on-line at:
www.peteblank.com

Printed in the United States of America

Copyright © 2012 Pete Blank
All rights reserved.

Library of Congress Control Number: 2012915283
ISBN-10: 144768705X
EAN-13: 9781477687055

What Others Are Saying About Employee Engagement – Lessons From the Mouse House

Employee engagement is common sense, but not common practice. Organizational leaders must operationalize this critical element to be recognized amongst the best performing organizations. And there's no better place to get best practices from than the Mouse House!

Claudio Diaz, SPHR
Chief Human Capital Officer
Wipfli LLP – one of the top 25 accounting and consulting firms in the nation

Leadership is a critical factor in today's corporate world but without loyal, focused followers there can be no true leader. Pete Blank shows leaders how to build an army of engaged employees who want to achieve new levels of achievement for their company, their industry, their leader and themselves.

Sean Carpenter
Director of Agent Development
Coldwell Banker, Columbus OH

The most important component to driving success and achieving positive outcomes in your business over the long term is ensuring that you maximize the level of employee engagement. Ambivalent and disengaged team members have a significant and detrimental effect to the bottom line. Need a recipe for success? Pete Blank hits these elements home in his entertaining yet simple and direct manner in his new book.

Robin Barca
Chief Operating Officer
Baptist Health, Montgomery AL

Employment Engagement is the key to increasing business results. Pete Blank comes from a high engagement culture at Walt Disney World. His views will benefit you as a leader and your organization's bottom line.

Rodney Miller
President
Smart Business Leadership, Franklin NC

To Sherri, my beautiful wife, thank you for choosing me.

To Madison and Logan, thank you for blessing me with smiles every day.

To God, thank you for your son Jesus Christ.

Acknowledgements

Writing a book is much harder than it seems. For the past five years, I have told hundreds of people that this book is coming.

The fact that it is finally here is a testament to many of my colleagues and friends.

Thanks to Brian Vagi, Kristin Palkovich and Merry Bise. You spent many hours with my first draft, and your edits have made this book more readable (I think...).

Thanks to the many Disney managers who helped share my passion for leadership: Adrianna Tibaudo, Laura Davis, Sandy Cordero, Lisa Downs, Michelle Reynolds and Wende Bendik. You kept *me* engaged every day for thirteen years.

Thanks to all the contributors who shared their stories of employee engagement. Your perspectives shine throughout this book and fill it with style and substance.

Finally, thanks to "the circle" for your enduring and never-ending friendship.

Table of Contents

Prologue and Caveats

To understand the content of this book, you need to understand the context of its author.

I am a Disney guy.

I can't help it. I love everything about Disney. I love their movies and their characters. I love their theme parks most of all. And I loved working at Walt Disney World. It was truly a marriage made in heaven.

I'd always wanted to work at Walt Disney World. I didn't know what I wanted to do, but I wanted to be there and get paid for it. In my mind the perfect job was a parade manager. I always thought the guys who walked at the end of the daily parade looked so cool. They always had radios in their hands, earpieces in their ears, and huge sets of keys clipped to their belts, *and* they always got to be at the end of the parade and wave to everyone. It must have been the power that attracted me.

It wasn't until college that I finally got my chance to work at the "mouse house." My older sister was married and living in Orlando, so I had a free place to live for the summer. I could keep all the money I made for three months and had very few expenses. But for me it wasn't about the money. It was about the chance to work for my dream company. Shoot—I would have worked there for free.

From June through August 1989, I worked in the Magic Kingdom's parking lot. That's right: the parking lot. Not the Magic Kingdom, not the Polynesian Resort, not even the monorails. The parking lot!

And I loved it.

That summer I learned about *guest service* —that you need to do everything in your power to create a great experience for your customers. I learned about *compromise*. For example when parking, no one liked to hear, "Go all the way down to the end of the row." These were *long* parking rows. If a customer missed the end spot near the tram by just one car, they'd be ticked off. Sometimes they'd be so ticked off they wouldn't go all the way down. They would just pull into another close spot, and I would have to stop all the incoming traffic until that person moved all the way down. But then I learned there was a time to do that, and there was a time just to let the guest park there and not worry about it.

I learned about *taking my job seriously*. When you're driving a tram engine pulling six passenger cars and approximately two hundred passengers, it's not a good idea to see how fast the tram will go on the back straight-away—especially when you have a secret shopper from the Florida Department of Transportation onboard, who then coaches you about safety in front of all the guests.

I learned about *teamwork*. It got up to ninety-nine degrees in the summer, but asphalt makes things hotter — much hotter! There were Gatorade buckets throughout the parking lot, but between the heat, the diesel fumes, and the regular gas fumes, headaches and fatigue were common. Fortunately there was always someone to jump in and help. I often heard, "I'll take your shift for a few — you take a quick break," and I learned to do the same for others.

I learned about having *passion for my job.* I was parking cars, driving trams, and spieling on the backs of trams — nothing glamorous. Yet I had a passion for it. Most of the people I worked with were happy to be there, and the feeling was contagious. Sure, some days were better than others, but most who worked in the parking lot loved it. They were there by choice.

I learned about *first contact*. The interactions we had with the guests could make or break the beginning of their day. I saw it all: people who opened their car doors as soon as they parked, and people who pulled in too close and crushed other people's car doors. I saw people locking their doors and leaving their keys in their running cars. I saw people in such a hurry to catch the tram they would run with a stroller under one arm and a crying kid under the other. It was our job to make sure we prepared them for the excitement that lay ahead.

Unfortunately, I had to take a break from Disney. After graduating from college, I moved to Birmingham, Alabama, to take a job as a sportscaster for a local CBS affiliate. I did that for two years and loved it — but not as much as I loved Disney.

I am a Disney guy.

In June 1994 my wife and I moved to Orlando so I could go back to work at Disney again. Let me share a quick story to explain how it used to be in Casting — what we called the recruiting and hiring department at Walt Disney World. In May 1994, when I began my career at Disney, Casting informed me they had no full-time roles with the exception of a bus driver. I was at the time a sportscaster in Birmingham, making between thirty and forty thousand dollars a year, and I had a college degree. I felt it was important to let Casting know this, yet their message remained the same.

However, they did let me know I could take one of many seasonal jobs, also known as *casual temporary* or CT, that were available, including one as a tour guide at The Great Movie Ride at Disney-MGM Studios. Then, if I performed well enough, I could try to move into a full-time role in August, when my CT role expired. (I found out later that my wife did not tell her parents this. The idea of leaving a well-paying TV job for a job with no benefits, no security, and low pay would not have gone over very well).

I did what most high-performing employees would do: I busted my butt, took all the overtime shifts no one wanted, did not complain, and volunteered to assist where needed. For three months I believed I was a perfect employee. About three weeks before my last official day as a seasonal worker, I went to my boss and asked if I could have a full-time job. While she checked and did everything she could, there were no openings. No one was leaving.

She told me to go and sell myself to the resorts side of the business, as there seemed to be more full-time openings there. So I put on my best suit, walked to three different hotels with resume in hand, and sold myself to any manager who would listen. I hit pay dirt when I met Steve Grace at Disney's Dixie Landings Resort. He and I immediately hit it off, and he invited me to become a part of the resort's team as a—you guessed it—CT cast member. Then, as soon as someone left, he would move me right into a full-time role.

Long story short, two months later I was a full-time cast member with all the benefits, and I was on my journey.

As a side note, Casting does not work that way anymore. With the opening of Disney's Animal Kingdom, Blizzard Beach water park, mini-golf courses, entertainment venues, and so on, Walt Disney World will never again have to deal with the possibility of being overstaffed and not having any openings.

The experience of being a CT taught me a great deal. My roles were many: attraction host at The Great Movie Ride at Disney-MGM Studios, front desk host at Dixie Landings Resort, bell services/front desk manager at Port Orleans Resort, and then multiple roles at Disney

University. For thirteen years I learned, laughed, and grew.

So why did I leave?

Simple: God first, family second, and I'm third. For thirteen years my in-laws would drive ten hours, stay twenty-four, and drive back ten more. As the kids came, the trips became more frequent. My mom passed away, and there were fewer and fewer of my family members in Florida. While my Disney coworkers were like family, I knew it was time to move our family back to Birmingham.

Although I have left Disney, Disney has never left me. I will always have a passion in my heart for that place and what it taught me. One of the main reasons I have that passion is the leaders I had the pleasure of working under. Every leader at Disney was always pushing for my best. They provided a work environment where I could succeed.

That is why I wanted to write this book. It's not easy keeping fifty employees engaged, let alone fifty thousand, which is how many of us there were when I left. The Walt Disney Company gave me so much in the way of leadership development and, in order to keep the dream alive, I wrote this book to share those lessons with you. While black and white text can never be a substitute for the experience of working at the largest single-site employer in the Southeastern US, I hope these stories and lessons will give you hope and inspiration to be the best leader you can be and create the best organization you can no matter where you work.

One of the reasons the Disney organization is so successful is its employees, or cast members. Disney lives off of the business model of cast-guest-business results: if you take care of the cast members, they will take care of the guests, which in turn is good for business. This is very simple and not exclusive to Disney. There's no business where you can just hire the employees, hand them the keys and radios, and tell them "good luck!" There's so much more to it, and it all starts with employee engagement — and that is what this book is about.

I would be remiss if I did not add a few disclaimers:

- The Disney way of doing business is not for everyone. There are many people out there who view Disney as they view Wal-Mart: they're both trying to take over the world. The hardest thing a true Disney fan can hear is his beloved company is just a business with stockholders, a board of directors, pension plans, and an operating budget the size of Manhattan. Somewhere between the fairy tales and the boardroom lies the truth.
- When you work for The Walt Disney Company, you are a part of a huge, moneymaking conglomerate. Translation: they have lots of resources available to them, including time, money, and people. Some of the processes you read about in this book may not be applicable to you, as you may have a small company, or you may work for the government or for a nonprofit. Keep in mind that the

lesson is for you to take what you can from this book and apply it to your organization.

- The information shared in this book is factual and accurate up to press time. As Disney is a living, breathing organization, some of the information in this book may have changed, updated, or been eliminated altogether since its publication.
- For the purposes of convenience and clarity, when I use the word *Disney* I am referring to The Walt Disney Company as a whole. When specifics are needed, I may also refer to Walt Disney World, Disneyland, Walt Disney (the man), and so on.

Now, let's get started and see what we can do to get you to add a little Disney magic to your organization.

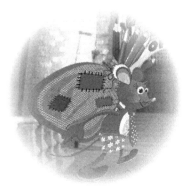

ONE
CHAPTER

ENGAGE THEM WITH EMPLOYEE DEVELOPMENT

> Keep the attractions staffed properly…
> never letting your personnel get sloppy…
> never let them be unfriendly.
>
> —*Walt Disney*

Before you can provide employees with the development they need, you need to know what *kind* of employee they are.

In April 2007, I began my second career as a training advisor in the Merit System of Jefferson County, Alabama. Although some people are called to a career

1

in government work, most seem to be in this business for the benefits or because they were referred by friends. Unsurprisingly, it's common to come across unhappy employees every now and then.

Disney has its share of those employees as well. If you think there are fifty thousand cast members in Orlando who love their jobs and think every day is filled with magic and pixie dust—well, let's just say your monorail doesn't go all the way to Tomorrowland.

For the most part, Disney has a very high ratio of happy or *engaged* cast members. For most of them, it can be summed up by one of four things: They love what they do (their JOB), they love the Disney brand (their ORGANIZATION), they love their manager (their BOSS), or they love the people they work with (their SQUAD).

If an employee fits in to just one of these quadrants, he or she will be OK; if not there will be trouble!

1. Love what you do (your JOB).

I had a cousin who worked at the now-defunct 20,000 Leagues Under the Sea attraction. He loved it. He loved the costume, he loved driving the submarines, he loved everything about the position. It didn't matter if his manager was good or bad. He loved driving a submarine regardless of the corporate culture around him. You will find this type of happy employee out there.

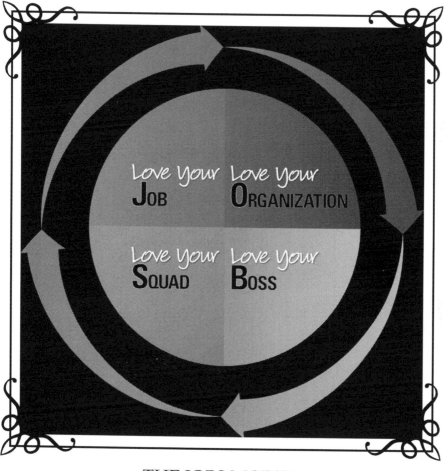

THE JOBS MODEL

The Disney parks have some job classifications that are unlike anything you will find anywhere in the world. There are Monorail pilots, Twilight Zone Tower of Terror bellhops, Jungle Cruise skippers, and Haunted Mansion hosts, just to name a few, and these jobs are just as fun as they sound. Are there some unhappy, cranky people working in these roles? Yes. But do you find others who are passionate about what they do? Yes again.

One of my first roles was as an attractions host at The Great Movie Ride at Disney's Hollywood Studios. Any extroverted comedian wannabe will tell you this is one of the greatest jobs on the property. You get to interact — literally — with Indiana Jones, James Cagney, and Dorothy from *The Wizard of Oz* on a daily basis. Also you get to interact with guests from all over the world, make them smile, and help them forget their worldly problems for twenty-two minutes. It really is a great job, and if I could have stayed there, I would have.

However, theme park jobs with fancy titles aren't the only ones with allure. You may hear the same thing from a pastry chef, an accountant, an HR manager, a custodial host, an EMT, or any other of the thousands of roles that are out there. Some people really just *like* their jobs. They're the ones you like to lead, and they're the ones who seem always to be engaged

2. Love your company (your ORGANIZATION).

There are employees who love everything Disney stands for. They know every fact about Walt Disney and are huge trivia buffs. For them it's not about the role—it's about the company.

These employees will refute all bad press and will not allow other employees to wax negatively about shrinking benefits, low salaries, or other realities about the company. They know Walt Disney had a dream to create a family-friendly theme park, and they feel like they're part of the plan to protect that dream.

Walt frequently walked though Disneyland talking with the cast members. He wanted to know what they liked, what they needed, and what would make their jobs easier. You might say Walt believed in the concept of MBWA, or management by walking around. That was how he determined what his employees needed.

3. Love your manager (your BOSS).

Imagine the following scenario: A manager asks his employees to stay late to clean the bathrooms and pick up the trash. The employees comply without concern. Why? Because they know he wouldn't ask them to do anything he wouldn't do himself. Simply put, they trust and respect their leader.

At Disney there's a lot of movement among leaders. In any organization you often find the best leaders stay in a location only a short time before they're whisked away to newer and greener pastures within the company. I've often heard stories about high-performing work locations that were the benchmarks for other departments until their leaders left. New leaders came in with new styles of leadership, and the departments were never the same.

During my time at Disney it wasn't uncommon to see cast members transfer to roles that were out of their comfort zones and expertise just to follow their leaders.

4. Love your coworkers (your SQUAD).

Some employees aren't as excited about the work they do, but they *are* excited about the people they get to work with. These employees could be working in any role at Disney and it would not matter as they are on a high-performing team and value workers over the work. This is especially true for the College Program interns. Early on, managers made the mistake of placing some of these interns in work environments where there were no other interns. It is well documented that members of Generation Y love to be around each other. They have a higher need for group interaction and dynamics.

Now that you have an idea which of the four quadrants is most representative of your employees, you're ready to shower them with training and career development opportunities. At Disney it was easy: We had Disney University (DU), where I spent the majority of my thirteen years. At Walt Disney World, the DU was an entire building behind the Magic Kingdom Park. At Disneyland it was a floor of the Team Disney building.

In actuality the entire Walt Disney World Resort is viewed as the world's largest experiential learning laboratory—a sort of large, living DU—which is an easy statement to make when you're blessed with more than thirty thousand acres. Let me share with you some ideas and concepts that originated in the DU. These are learning and development opportunities you can offer your employees, and you don't need a corporate university to implement them.

Create an employee resource center

While I was at Walt Disney World (WDW), the employee resource center went though many different brandings. At one time it was called Centers of Excellence, and each theme park and resort had one. Then it was rebranded as Disney Learning Centers. Depending on space these centers had computers, books, DVDs and videos, magazines, and quiet sitting areas. Cast members used them during their breaks and before and after shifts.

Because of the diverse cast, many activities occurred in these resource centers. Cast members took e-learning courses, checked out books and magazines, came in for resume help, and used the computers to work on their English-speaking skills—all at no cost to them. This was part of what was called the *Disney Difference*.

The sizes of the resource areas differed. The main center at the Disney University was by far the largest, whereas Disney's Port Orleans Resort center had a small room with two or three computers and a few books. However, employee usage was always high regardless of the size. Staffing was a minimal cost; even the bigger areas employed just a few cast members, and the smaller centers just unlocked the doors and used the honor system.

If you plan to open an employee resource center, there are five important items for you to remember:

1. Branding: make every effort to create a center that is inviting and enjoyable. Lighting, music, decorations, and furniture must reflect your brand and image. No one wants to spend time in the closet down the hall with two computers and dusty, old furniture.

2. Hours: what type of hours you're your organization have? If you run three shifts over twenty-four hours, but your center is open only from 8:00 a.m. to 5:00 p.m., two of your three shifts may be dissatisfied. Make sure your center is available to all employees during their working hours.

3. Content: remember, everything is electronic these days, and you don't want your employee resource center becoming a dinosaur before it even opens. It shouldn't be a dumping ground for old training manuals and donated romance novels. Stock it with computers. Provide laptop stations and free coffee and sodas. Purchase several e-readers and have them available for employees to check out.

4. Employee input: you have to ensure your employees have a say in this space. How would they use

it? To learn? To veg out? To socialize and meet friends? Make it a true flex space—don't let it become dead space.

5. Management support: why would you spend money on this? I guarantee your CFO is going to want to see the return on investment. Is it a recruiting tool or a retention tool? Is it a cost center that fits your brand as a company and supports lifelong learning? These are questions you will want to have answered before you're asked.

Showcase your employee success stories

Do you want to see your employees engaged? Then show them there are abundant opportunities for upward mobility. In my experience in local government, I find that some employees may feel stuck when it comes to career advancement. The employees who want to move forward in their careers find incumbents who have no intention of leaving the jobs they want.

WDW is much different. There was an attraction at Epcot for many years called Horizons, which was sponsored by GE. On the wall at the entrance of the attraction was the phrase *If you can dream it, you can do it...* When it comes to establishing career paths at Disney, this holds true.

When I arrived at Disney in 1994, I was told the internal promotion rate was about 90-10, which meant 90 percent of promotions were internal, while 10 percent were hired from outside the organization. When I left Disney in 2007, the number was more along the lines of 70-30. Still, that's an amazing amount of opportunity for internal growth and promotion.

I am a perfect example, as I had a degree in telecommunications with TV broadcasting experience when I began at WDW in attractions. From there I moved to a resort front desk, became a bell services manager, was cross-utilized as an orientation consultant, and then became a manager on that team. I was moved to teach a college-level curriculum to college interns, then I designed and developed professional development classes for the entire company. Not bad for a guy who began by parking cars in the Magic Kingdom.

My advice to you is to make sure your employees hear the success stories of those who have made their way around your company. Notice that I used the word *around* rather than *up*. Disney uses a model that envisions climbing the corporate *latticework* as opposed to a corporate *ladder*. This essentially means there is more than one way to get to the top, and sometimes it requires moving left, right, and even down before moving up. And that's OK. As long as your employees aren't stuck in their current roles or at their current levels, they will work hard for you. When they're told there's nowhere to go, they'll stop performing at their highest levels.

Bryan Quick was a recruiter for Walt Disney World and is currently the training director at the Lincoln Park Zoo in Chicago. Once of these latticework roles he applied for was as a WDW ambassador. The Ambassador Program traces its roots all the way back to Walt Disney himself. As Disneyland Park was growing, Walt was having trouble meeting all the demands on him for press interviews, public relations needs, and so on, so he created the program, where a current cast member is selected to represent the company for one year. During that time the ambassador attends functions, speaks publicly about the company, attends employee recognition events, and generally embodies the Disney brand. When Walt Disney World opened in 1971, the program was instituted there as well. It is a program in which Bryan was very interested:

> I remember the first interaction I had with a Disney ambassador and how passionate they were about the heritage of the company and how they seemed to live and breathe Walt's vision. I was greatly impacted by this; it defined the next fourteen years of my career with Disney, including representing the organization as a recruiter.
>
> Later, toward the last half of those years, I had a phenomenal leader who was truly committed to my development. She believed I too could be an ambassador. She pushed me each year to learn more, motivating me and mentoring me—as well as consoling me when I fell short of being selected.
>
> During my final two years at Disney, I was proud to be a quarterfinalist in the Walt Disney World

BRYAN QUICK OUTSIDE THE FLAGSHIP PARK
OF WALT DISNEY WORLD RESORT, DISNEY'S
MAGIC KINGDOM

Ambassador Program. There have been very few moments in my life that made me feel more a part of something than that. There are a lot of good leaders out there, but the few who make the most of the time they have with you are the great ones. This principle has guided me many times in my interactions with people I manage and develop.

– Bryan Quick

I understand his passion. In 2003 I also applied to be a WDW ambassador. Although I was not selected, the experience added to my leadership toolkit, and the partnerships I made were invaluable.

Opportunities like cross-utilization's and the Ambassador Program were all part of the My Disney Career (MDC) concept. Actually, MDC was the platform brand for multiple strategic outlets, including posters, a website, and a conference.

Being promoted from within is one of the many benefits of working for Disney. Al Weiss, who was the president of WDW during my tenure, began his career as an hourly cast member in cash control. His job was to zero out the registers after the Magic Kingdom closed each night. While it's unlikely that many employees will follow a similar career track, there are four ways you can let them know what they can do to find success in your organization.

1. Get the message out: Gather your employees who have worked their way up, down, and around into positions of success, and share their stories

with others. You can start a poster campaign in your hallways, create a website, or ask successful employees to give "lunch and learn" presentations on what they did to move from position to position. Whatever you decide to do, the most important part is getting them out there to share.

2. Be honest: If there is no room for movement, don't keep it a secret! In my government job, we have about sixty employees. One division employs about twenty-two workers and one manager who isn't going anywhere for a while. Don't sell your company as something it isn't, and be sure to set up expectations during the hiring process.

3. Create a networking fair: If you have a big company with lots of lateral movement, this might be a hit with your employees. Set up a large classroom as if it were a conference or expo hall for several hours. Man each booth with individuals from different lines of business to share information about what they do and how to get into their line of work.

   For example we had lots of attractions cast members and many food-and-beverage cast members who wanted to transfer into other areas at Disney but didn't know what was out there. Let's say Joe had an undergraduate degree in marketing but worked in a hotel until he could figure out how to get into his area of expertise. A networking fair would allow him to meet people in the marketing department, exchange business cards, and talk about action plans. It's a great win for both the department hosting the booth and the employee.

4. Emphasize education: Either your organization supports formal degrees or it doesn't. Find out what your company's stance is, then support it. If it's pro-education (which it should be, by the way), then it should offer educational reimbursement opportunities and hold annual education fairs. One is high cost and one is low cost, but both share the same message with the employees: we care about you, and we want you to succeed, gain knowledge, and help our company grow. We want you to become a better employee.

Education fairs are quite easy to organize. Just contact local community colleges, trade and vocational schools, online universities that may have presences in your location, and the local universities. Set a date, advertise, set up tables, and watch the magic happen. Most colleges and universities have representatives who love to attend educational fairs and usually bring plenty of giveaways and door prizes, which will help encourage attendance.

Make sure it's an all-day event so individuals working all shifts can stop by, and make sure you host it at a central location with convenient parking for employees and guests. Those of you with higher budgets may want to provide box lunches for the school representatives.

The first booth all attendees should visit is your educational reimbursement booth, where you can distribute copies of your company's policy so your employees understand how to take advantage of this opportunity. I received my master's in human resources from Rollins College while I worked at Disney. The entire degree cost around $14,000, and I think I paid about $300 out of pocket. Talk about creating an engaged employee!

Sarah Gaffney is an employee who felt connected to the Disney organization due to her educational opportunities. We worked together at the Disney University, and now she's a program coordinator at Florida Atlantic University.

But her exciting story comes from when she worked in business relations at Downtown Disney:

> My leader during this time, Troy Talpas, played a critical role in my professional and personal growth and development. If I were to summarize briefly Troy's leadership strengths that enabled my success, it would be in three words: SUPPORT, ENCOURAGEMENT, and EMPOWERMENT. He helped me see my potential!
>
> While working with Troy at Downtown Disney, his support, encouragement, and trust to empower me

SARAH GAFFNEY MAKES MAGIC THROUGH
SWEET TREATS AT DOWNTOWN DISNEY

as an employee catapulted me to a new level in my career. Under his leadership I returned to school and completed my bachelor's degree, successfully participated in a task force that coordinated the opening of Downtown Disney, Anaheim, and obtained a promotion to my first leadership role with Disney.

Rather than trying to groom me or manage me as an employee, Troy took the time to take an interest and ask about my goals, then did all he could to help me achieve them. This is how I believe a true leader performs—an exceptional leader. I should also note he even drove three hours to attend my graduation celebration when I completed my degree!

I can honestly say that without Troy's leadership I would not have had the amount of professional success I have. To this day I encounter situations in which I think, *What would Troy do?* To this day his leadership guides me to success!

— Sarah Gaffney

Troy's leadership style is not unusual at Disney. By supporting employees and their academic achievements, he creates a higher-performing and extremely dedicated workforce.

Provide exciting and relevant traditional classroom training

If you want to engage your employees, you need to provide dynamic training opportunities that relate to their professional development. Sure, we all have to attend OSHA and workplace harassment trainings. But mandatory trainings do not engage employees. You need to provide consistent, ongoing leadership, customer service, and professional development training.

Here are some tips to get you started or to improve what you have:

1. Be aware of the power of supervisors: There is nothing worse than when excited and engaged employees who want to attend trainings are told they can't go because they're needed in the operation, or because it would not be fair to the other employees who cannot attend, or because they have not been there long enough, or the hundreds of other reasons management can claim. The real reason why operations managers say "no" to training is it creates more work for *them*. They have to adjust schedules, change workflow, or cover shifts. It's easier for them just to tell everyone they can't go. If you have leaders like this in your organization, you need to coach them on the relevance of training.

   Another reason managers may not want to send their employees is they do not see the value of training. Sometimes when employees return from customer service training, they continue in their old ways and do not activate any type of behavior change. Therefore the managers see no reason to continue to send people, and they come to regard training as a waste of time.

   Is the problem here with the employee or the leader? There's an old saying: "You cannot send a changed person back to an unchanged environment." The manager needs to reflect on this and decide where the issue lies. Perhaps the problem is with the culture, but it's possible it's with the training department, and that leads us to the next solution.

2. Make sure you have the right people leading your classes. As a professional trainer, I tend to be a bit of a training snob, but there is no mistaking the importance of a qualified facilitator to lead your most important asset: your employees!

   I also support the concept of employing leaders as teachers — that is, using your leadership team members as facilitators. Remember, though, it will dampen your training brand if they stand behind a podium and deliver monotone monologues rather than open dialogues. To prevent this, be sure you have a good "train the trainer" class in place. Have a qualified facilitator share the importance of classroom management with the instructors. Neither managers nor employees will see the value of training if they do not learn something, have fun, and apply it back at work!

Provide an internal conference

This may be more relevant to larger organizations — it worked well for Disney.

Sending hundreds of employees to conferences, with hotel and travel costs, can be easily offset by having an internal conference. Bringing in a few keynote speakers and using your internal talent to lead breakout sessions is more cost effective than paying for conference registrations, plane fares, and hotel accommodations for all of your employees. WDW started its annual leadership conference in the mid-2000s. However, it was designed for only management, and the hourly cast members felt left out. Because Disney listens, they created the Showcase of Opportunities, which carried plenty of sessions on career development for the non-salaried employees. Just remember the time and effort to create this must be balanced with an actual return on investment

Train for fun

As an employee wouldn't it be great if your organization offered some training and development that had nothing to do with work? For the company the only returns would be the employees' happiness and feelings of being valued.

That's where this idea comes in. Why not create quarterly trainings on topics such as how to use Facebook, wine tasting, photography, guitar lessons, or starting a blog? There is a chance your local community college or trade school already offers classes like these, so they would be easy to implement. Some community colleges might offer tuition discounts, or may even bring the sessions to your workplace. This tells your employees you care about them and want to do something nice for them.

Putting it all together

At the end of the day, employee engagement can be directly linked to employee development. If you choose just one of the ideas above and implement it, chances are you will improve employee morale and retention levels.

When all is said and done, you may never know the positive impact you have on your employees. As leaders we spend ample time coaching and developing our employees — sometimes without thanks, but that's not why we do it. We lead and develop them because we know the value that each and every employee can bring to the organization.

Malcolm Stevens was a guest service manager for Future World West Attractions in Epcot. Although he now works in a ministry, he always had a heart for developing his team — and you can see that clearly in these words from one of his former employees:

> I worked with Malcolm during the year 2002 at the Magic Kingdom in Orlando, Florida. While Malcolm and I did not work in the same area of the park all that often, I can say with complete confidence that Malcolm practiced the highest level of guest service in his role as area manager. What I admire about Malcolm is his work ethic and ability to fulfill the expectations of his role. Disney provides a list of seven keys to maintaining guest service satisfaction, and Malcolm not only practiced these keys at all times but was a leader to all cast members in and under his role.

During Disney's Nights of Joy, I would greet Malcolm in front of the castle, and other cast members would be following him, ready to answer the call of need wherever it would arise. This is a clear sign of leadership, because not only did other cast members respect Malcolm as their leader, but they also maintained a great sense of order in front of their him. A great deal of respect must be earned to command such a display of order.

I will never forget the moment of urgency I experienced on one particular day. I was in a panic and needed immediate assistance to remedy a problem. Malcolm called me on the phone. I casually answered, "Hey, man." Before I could get any further into the conversation, Malcolm interrupted to remind me I needed to answer professionally because anyone could have been on the other end of the line. Wow! A man who could be honest and strict at any time during his workday! I have to be honest—I was taken aback at first, but I look back on that moment and realize Malcolm was providing me with great advice that proved valuable in my own professional career.

After Malcolm and I finished our conversation, he came to my location with two other cast members, and together we fixed the issue in little time. Again, a strong sense of order!

What I most admire in Malcolm when it comes to guest service is his vibrant attitude. As most people will tell you, a smile goes a long way. Malcolm excels at social interaction, and while he might not be Mickey or Goofy, his friendly nature often made guests' days. Sure, I didn't always chat with guests after their conversations with Malcolm, but you don't

MALCOLM STEPHENS (MIDDLE) WITH HIS TEAM
AT DOWNTOWN DISNEY

have to guess how they feel when you see them walk away with smiles on their faces.

My friendship with Malcolm is one that I cherish and thank God for. I love it, man! Once a few of us cast members got together after a workday to have a group prayer. Malcolm shone so bright; his energy alone is powerful. I'm always so inspired when someone can say a prayer of thanks, and Malcolm did that and more. In a moment of impromptu fellowship, he said a prayer of passion with such eloquence I figured he must have practiced it!

What I love most about Malcolm is his celebratory attitude when he hears about how God is working in the lives of others. If I were to compare it to anything, I would say it was like watching your son on Christmas morning when he opens the exact gift he wanted. But with Malcolm the emotions run much deeper and are outwardly focused—a quality all admire.

If I had one complaint, I would say this: I wish I could have given back the amount I received from Malcolm. I would describe our relationship in the context of Proverbs 27:17—"Iron sharpeneth iron; so a man sharpeneth the countenance of his friend." But the thing is, I don't feel like my iron has sharpened Malcolm's in the same way. I don't put myself down over it, though. Instead I thank the Lord for Malcolm's inspiration because it creates motivation, and it commands that I share a similar kindness and wisdom with my friends and family.

When Malcolm read this account, he responded by stating, "For me it was heartwarming to hear of the impact I had on a young man, especially with regard to an event I had long forgotten." As a leader who develops employees, you have more power than you will ever know.

Now it's your turn! What can you do to keep your employees engaged? Use the worksheet on the next page to create three action items you can implement regarding employee development.

Action Items for Chapter One: Employee Development

List three things you can do to create more developmental opportunities for your employees:

#1

#2

#3

CHAPTER

ENGAGE THEM VIA TEAM BUILDING

The whole thing here is the organization.
Whatever we accomplish belongs to our entire group,
a tribute to our combined effort...
Everything here at Disneyland and the studio
is a team effort.

—*Walt Disney*

As a trainer in local government, clients frequently ask me to come out to their city/department/jurisdiction and help them fix what they call their *employee problems* — or, put another way, their problem employees. They tell me their people are not providing good customer service and want me to give a refresher class.

29

What happens in these classes does not surprise me anymore. After some Q/A and feedback sessions, I come to realize the employees don't have any problems providing adequate customer service; they just don't want to. And most of the time it's because they hate their bosses/leaders/fellow employees. One city employee actually told me, "Pete, I know how to give good service. I just hate the people I work with, and that makes me not want to be here."

To me that is fascinating information. You will recall that in chapter one we talked about the JOBS Model – Love your Job, Love your Organization, Love your Boss, and Love your Squad. When your employees intensely dislike each other, the problem could be that they're working side by side with a bunch of numbskulls. The more likely scenario, however, is that there's very little team building happening in the area.

Employee conflict is inevitable, but it may lead to positive changes. Though coworkers may argue and bicker over policies and strategies, if they respect each other success can be the result. When there is no respect between peers and the conflict is over who gets the good cubicle or who gets to go to lunch first, you have a recipe for disaster.

Let's look at some ways to promote team building.

Use a team building profile

There are plenty of examples out there, from the Myers-Briggs Type Indicator (MBTI), which is based on personalities, to the DiSC profile, which helps with communication skills, and a host of others. Sometimes the easiest answer to team building is assisting the team members with understanding each other. Yes, electronic or hard-copy profiles cost money, but so do the sick days employees take due to high stress or conflict avoidance.

Have a team day, a team lunch, or an offsite team meeting

I know the hardcore bottom-line managers do not like to hear this, but it's true: today's employees needs more than just work to keep them engaged. Whether it's a scheduled event or a spur-of-the-moment movie, employees need to spend time together during work hours. The worst thing you can do when attempting to build a team is to schedule an event at 5:00 p.m. on a Friday, or a team picnic on a Saturday afternoon. You'll kill the team with this style of activity. Do what you can to allow the events to happen at work while on the clock.

At Disney this was simple. All you had to do was get your team, head over to a theme park, and go on a few rides for fun. I realize now how blessed we were to have that option at our fingertips. Still, there are plenty of options for your team. For example go to a movie, a local tourist attraction, a museum, or a restaurant.

AMY KESMAN ROSSI ACTING A LITTLE *GOOFY*
AT DISNEY'S CALIFORNIA ADVENTURE

Maybe all you need is some quiet time alone with your team, away from any and all distractions. Amy Kesman Rossi was a project development consultant for Disney's PhotoPass with Operations Learning & Development. Currently she is the training manager for the Union League Club of Chicago. She still remembers the impact her leader had on her when it came to team building:

> My favorite team-building experience happened regularly when my manager Cindy and I were a mighty team of two. When we both needed a break, we would each get a cup of tea and sit in her office for a couple of hours, talking about anything and everything. We would start with our current projects and hop from tangent to tangent until we felt like we could take on the world again. Sometimes we even went out into the park for Mickey Premium Bars!
>
> The beauty of being on a two-person team was that we could both recognize when the other needed a break and could talk each other back in from the ledge when necessary. Team building became a natural part of our work relationship, and she and I are friends to this day!
>
> — *Amy Kessman Rossi*

As you can see, not all team building has to include theme-park rides, lunches, and other costly avenues. Sometimes a quiet space, a little time, and a cup of tea can do wonders for your team spirit.

Use your internal partners

First of all you may have to partner with other departments. For example, when I worked at Dixie Landings front desk, I would occasionally be scheduled to work shifts at our sister resort, Port Orleans. This allowed the Port Orleans front desk team to take a few hours to engage in team-building activities. Then, later in the year, they would do the same for us.

Do you have other departments where you could create this plan? If you have already built the relationships, it's easy to get your partners to assist. At Disney we would call our partners in the recreation department and ask to borrow a couple of pontoon boats for two hours to go fishing. We also called our partners at the campground and asked to borrow a cabin for a team meeting, and our partners in the theme parks to borrow unused restaurants as a meeting space in the morning. All of those options cost us nothing! Granted, Walt Disney World has seemingly unlimited resources to choose from, but if you're good at relationships, you should be able to do this as well. Who do you know? Where do they work? And what can you barter to provide your team with an opportunity to bond?

Use your external partners

You may have a small business with few internal partners. So you may have to look outside your organization. You can start with the church you attend, professional organizations you belong to, or chambers of commerce where your employees may be members.

The key is to get the conversations started, then set up reciprocal agreements.

In my local government job, we've partnered with a local historic theater that is usually only booked for nighttime events. They let us use the 2,500-seat theater for an extremely low price, and threw in cans of soda and boxes of popcorn. We watched a private showing of *We Are Marshall* followed by a debriefing session on what we learned. The team just loved it, and the catchphrase of the movie ("We ARE Marshall!") is still mentioned when teams succeed. Don't say you can't do this. You're only limited by your imagination and creativity.

Create a fun working environment

The leader is responsible for setting the tone of the office. If the leader hates Mondays, dislikes every policy, and feels like the company is off track, then his employees will follow.

Conversely, if the leader works with a smile, provides good, clean fun and laughter, and creates an environment where people smile, efficiency and productivity is bound to improve. Lisa Downs was the best at this. As my manager for many years, she knew how important it was to have fun. After all we worked at Walt Disney World. All the guests were having fun — why shouldn't we?

LISA DOWNS (BACK RIGHT) LEADS HER COLLEGE
PROGRAM TEAM WITH FUN, FUN, FUN!

Although she's now the manager of Disney Internships and Programs, she was the team leader for the Traditions Program at Disney University. She made sure that team had fun:

> For about six to nine months, we were addicted to this game called Bop-it! It was a handheld game that gave commands you had to perform before handing it off to the next person.
>
> You could call this out-of-the-box team building, but this is a fun toy I believe both relieved stress and built my team! We worked in an operation that, like most areas, became very stressful at times. When I could see people were reaching their breaking points, or we just needed some fun, I would gather the team and call Bop-it time! The team gathered in a circle and played the game for five minutes. We laughed, we talked, we did a silly dance and cheer... then went back to work! It doesn't really matter what the game is. It's about being silly, taking five minutes to bond, and making memorable moments for teams. I've always had the motto of "work hard, play harder," and I still receive e-mails today about our Bop-it time... Oh, and a disco ball glowing while you're playing never hurts!
>
> – Lisa Downs

I still have fun working for the government, and I try every day to help my peers understand that they can have fun at work. In fact, it should be required!

Putting it all together

Now it's your turn! What can you do to keep your employees engaged? Use the worksheet on the next page to create three action items you can implement regarding team building.

Action Items for Chapter Two: Team Building

List three things you can do to create more team-building opportunities for your employees:

#1

#2

#3

ᴛHREE
CHAPTER

ENGAGE THEM THROUGH MOTIVATION

Happiness is a state of mind.
It's just according to the way you look at things.
So I think happiness is contentment,
but it doesn't mean you have to have wealth.

—*Walt Disney*

Different people are motivated by different things

I wish I had known and understood that statement before my first supervisory job.

Most supervisors believe a good salary, job security, and promotion and growth are the most important factors that motivate employees. The reality is employees want a leader who gives them full appreciation for work done and lets them feel like they're in on things.

Why the disconnect? One reason is the supervisor's choice is easier.

- It's easy to give a good salary or defend a poor one ("times are tough," "I don't control the purse strings").
- It's easy to offer job security ("if you do a good job and keep your nose clean, you will always have a home here").
- It's easy to offer promotions and growth opportunities.

But give employees appreciation? That takes work. So does letting them feel in on things. If there's one thing I have learned about mediocre managers, it's that they do *not* want to hear about their employees' personal problems.

In my current job, three county employees clean our building. Recently, due to budget cuts and the economy, their hours were cut from forty to thirty-two, in effect giving each of them a third day off during the week. Well, there were three people vying for the two most desirable days off — Monday and Friday — which meant someone would get stuck with split days off. According to the above graph, a successful leader would ask the three employees how they wanted to handle it. Perhaps they could work out a rotation schedule. Or, in a worse case, the supervisor could go by seniority and let the two highest-ranking employees get the Mondays and Fridays, and let the lowest employee pick Tuesdays, Wednesdays, or Thursdays.

Again, employees appreciate having a say. But all that is too much work for the manager, so what does he do? One person gets Tuesday off, one Wednesday, and one Thursday. No controversy, and less work for the supervisor. Also a very uncaring and non-motivational way to decide! You can just about guarantee motivation and morale will be low for these employees for quite some time.

Part of the problem is the coexistence of the terms *motivation* and *recognition*. While they are not mutually exclusive, I prefer to cover them separately. For the purposes of this book, this chapter will only focus on the concept of *motivating* your employees. You can read more about *recognition* in chapter five.

Dave Ramsey tells a great story of motivation in his seminars. In a university study completed in the mid-1960s, unemployed workers were hired to dig a ditch all day for pay that was *higher* than minimum wage. The thought was that they would be ecstatic to have this great job in a poor economy that paid so well.

In the morning of day one, they were told to dig a ditch. After lunch they were told to fill the ditch back in. On day two they all returned and were told to dig a ditch again. Halfway through day two, they were told fill the ditch back in.

Before they left after day two, they were told that if they returned for day three to do it again, their pay would be doubled. Forty percent did not show up. The lesson was simple: it doesn't matter how much you pay people to work; there has to be a sense of purpose and fulfillment in everyday jobs. There has to be meaning to what people are doing in life. There are plenty of training videos and books out there right now that deal with this topic.

You could be happy working with dirty fish all day, and you could be happy driving a bus all day. The end-all question has to do with intrinsic versus extrinsic motivation. If your employees are intrinsically motivated, chances are they're also engaged employees. If they know what it takes to get themselves up and going, to put in the hours, to work for the good of the company, to always do the right thing, then you're in good shape. Perhaps you're one of those people too.

The challenge comes with employees who need to be motivated by something externally. Some employees need thank you notes, gift cards, verbal praise and so on to feel validated.

Julie Couret Willoz is a faculty member at Tulane University, but I knew her when she was a regional recruiter for the Disney College and CareerStart Programs. She understood that for employees, *motivation* just meant having a leader who was available:

JULIE WILLOZ, MONORAIL PILOT AND MANAGER
EXTRAORDINAIRE

Summers are hot in Orlando, and the 1977 polyester costume did not make it any cooler for the Monorail pilots. As a guest service manager, I sought always to recognize and thank my drivers for providing a safe and fun experience.

I made my rounds through all the stations to engage with and observe the drivers, always looking for them doing their best. I would award them with a Guest Service Fanatic card and be sure to tell them I knew they did more than I ever saw for the guests. Monorails had cast members who had been with the company and in that location for five, ten, fifteen, even twenty years! As their manager I trusted, supported, and appreciated each and every driver. I complimented their efforts in front of other drivers and guests. If a driver sought to gain more responsibility, I would work to see that happen.

My gratitude for what they did for the guests and for the Walt Disney World Resort was sincere. I certainly do not take all the credit for their great work, but I do believe my support helped them through the long and hot days.

– Julie Willoz

Just being available and saying "thank you" may be what it takes to prevent unmotivated employees.

I first came into contact with unmotivated employees at Disney's Port Orleans Resort, when I accepted my first supervisory role. I was to be a guest service manager, and I was ready to shake up the world. As a bellman at that same resort, I'd been peers with many great cast members, and with some actively disengaged ones.

When I was promoted, I truly could not wait to have an impact on these employees.

I mistakenly believed all I had to do was lead by example, and everyone would soon follow. I came to work on time, I left late, I was never angry or cross, I spoke politely with all the angry guests in the lobby, and I tried to spread the Disney magic through my work.

Nothing happened.

I tried a different approach. If I couldn't motivate them with my actions, then I would do it with my words. Each of the four guest service managers was assigned a homeroom with fifteen to twenty cast members apiece. This gave each cast member one main supervisory contact for things like performance reviews, one-on-one coaching, and so on.

I named my group Pete's Pals, and we met about every other week. I began each session with a stirring lesson, a successful guest service interaction, and a thought for the week.

Strike two.

So now I was stumped. If I could not motivate them with my words, and I could not motivate them with my actions, what was I to do? My personal goals would not allow me to let them flounder and fail. How was I to avoid strike three?

"Different people are motivated by different things."

Most of you already knew the answer—it just took me a little while to get it. The bottom line is that people cannot be motivated extrinsically until they decide they are ready to be motivated — an intrinsic feeling of motivation, so to speak.

I realized I had to spend time with all of my employees to find out where they were on their career paths and what motivated them. I'll give you some real-life action items below that will guide you as you try to get your employees motivated.

- **Decide what to do with the bottom 10 percent.**
  As a leader it is your responsibility to have a direction when it comes to your low performers. If you are Jack Welch of GE, you fire them all. Not all of us have the gumption, stamina, or staffing levels to do that.

  Another option is to spend more time with them. Actively disengaged employees who are not motivated are a recipe for disaster. If you do not take control of them, they will take control of you and their fellow employees. Therefore you might want to set aside weekly one-on-one time for them until they understand your expectations.

  A final option may be just to ignore them. Understand that every department has a bottom 10 percent and there is nothing you can do about it. Place them in jobs that have zero guest interaction, and let them flounder away their days until retirement. Hold them accountable, and use progressive discipline, but don't try to motivate them. Some employees will always be unhappy.

As you can imagine, I am not a proponent of this final option, but each of you has your own problem employee and know what is best. One thing you do *not* want to do is transfer your un-motivated employee for the sole reason of passing him or her off to someone else. That is one of the worst hypocrisies of leadership. "I have a terrible employee that I have failed to fix, so I'm dumping him on you." Transferring an unmotivated employee is okay if it's for the right reasons, and if the other location is up to the task. But don't send your dirty laundry to my house for me to wash it—I have enough of my own

- **Communicate your expectations clearly on day one.** Another reason why employees are not mo-tivated to come to work and do their best is they have never been told what is expected of them. All employees have their own expectations of their jobs, and those expectations need to match up with the department's, company's, or man-ager's expectations. When the two do not meet, there is bound to be conflict.

   Your employees need to know, in the simplest terms, what you expect from them. For example, "I expect you will always be on time, I expect you will always do your best to assist guests, and I expect you will come to me, your leader, whenever you have an issue and want to talk."

At Walt Disney World, we used expectations to simplify the needs of both the guests and the cast members. Our four guest expectations were:

o Make me feel special.
o Treat me as an individual.
o Respect me and my children.
o Be knowledgeable.

Through exit surveys and focus groups, Disney realized that if all of its cast members tried to fulfill these guest expectations, there would be higher satisfaction ratings and lower complaints.

There were also four cast expectations:

o Make me feel special.
o Treat me as an individual.
o Respect me.
o Make me knowledgeable.

As you can see, the cast member expectations are eerily similar to the guest expectations. And why shouldn't they be? If you really want your employees to be motivated, you need to make sure there are simple, effective expectations in place.

While there is no order of importance placed on these, I personally feel that "treat me like an individual" may be the most valued. Some leaders don't always take full advantage of this one. In my current job, we had a building housekeeper, Mary (not her real name), who was the nicest person and the most efficient when it came to cleanliness. Her primary job was to empty trash cans, vacuum, and do general light housekeeping.

She'd had this job for more than twenty years, and I enjoyed the witty banter we shared daily. She was particularly fond of her grandchildren. In fact one of them was graduating from kindergarten, and she was looking forward to attending the event. Now, I've attended both of my children's kindergarten graduations, and I agree it seems silly to have all these five-year-olds wearing caps and gowns. But the kids like it, and the adults like it, and it seems to be a rite of passage.

It turns out that Mary asked her boss if she could leave work for about two hours to attend. Her boss said she could not, and cited many reasons—she was out of vacation time for that year, and so on. So Mary did what most grandparents would have done: she went anyway. Upon her return the next day, she was fired.

I do not condone insubordination. However, neither do I condone poor decision making, and that leader made a poor decision. This was a great employee who went above and beyond and is now gone. And by the way, the building is not as clean as it used to be, and definitely not as much fun.

- **Make full use of your company's probationary period.** Some say motivation ebbs and flows like the tide—some days you have it, and some days you don't. However, if I watch an employee over a week's time, I can tell if she is going to have what it takes. If she does not, let her go. I don't care if the probationary period is six days, six weeks, or six months. Any of them is plenty of time to monitor and evaluate your employees. If they do not seem motivated to be at work, let them go, and find somebody who is. Motivated people are out there. Trust me.

Putting it all together

Now it's your turn! What can you do to increase motivation in your workplace? Use the worksheet on the next page to create three action items you can implement regarding motivation.

Action Items for Chapter Three: Motivation

List three things you can do to motivate your employees:

#1

#2

#3

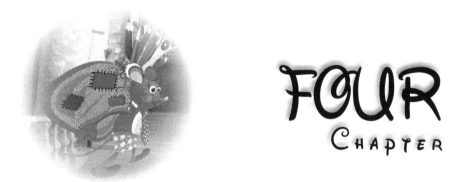

FOUR

Engage Them by Enhancing Your Leadership Skills

Courage is the main quality of leadership,
in my opinion, no matter where it is exercised.

—Walt Disney

While we spent the first three chapters examining what *employees* need to do about engagement, it would be hypocritical if I did not remind you that the apple does not fall far from the tree. As the leader goes, so goes the employee. You need to make sure *you* are engaged in your role as a leader.

First some terminology. At Disney everyone is a leader, which can make for some very confusing dialogue. That's right—every employee is considered to be in a leadership role. It begins at local orientation and oozes throughout the culture. Yes, there are managers and bosses and supervisors and even proprietors (at Disney's Animal Kingdom), and they are titled as leaders, but every employee is expected to act and behave as a leader.

What does that mean? It means everyone's opinion is valued. Everyone is allowed to have input in their area because fifty thousand viewpoints are a lot better than one, or ten, or a hundred. The corporate culture allows this leadership concept to flourish. Titles are granted, but leadership is earned through respect and trust. One wrong decision or move can have a devastating impact on employee engagement.

On the other hand, the hierarchical view of leadership is alive and well in local government. It's as far from the Disney culture as you can imagine. There is a person at the top, and he or she makes the decisions regarding what is best. Anyone who comes with a new or different idea is sometimes branded as a rebel and non-team player, and may be left out of promotional talk. It truly is a political game.

As a leadership trainer in government, most of my class participants are front-line leaders, and they're trying to have positive impacts in their workplaces. But when their excitement is squashed and shut down, a lack of engagement is sure to follow.

How is leadership viewed in your work environment? Is there an expectation of leadership from everyone, or is it for the chosen few?

John Maxwell once said, "Leadership is influence. Nothing more, nothing less." There is no better way to influence the people you lead than by performing the role of leader every day in every situation. One of the biggest mistakes a leader can make is being a hypocrite. "Do as I say, not as I do" may work in parenting but will disconnect you from your staff and minimize your level of influence.

In order to be a successful leader, I have designed what I call the R.O.L.E. Model of Leadership. Relationships, Oversight, Leverage and Evolvement. I will cover the concepts of Relationships and Leverage in chapter six. However, step two, Oversight, is a great stepping off point for our discussion of leadership skills.

A successful leader needs to have oversight of his or her physical environment. Employees will only follow a leader who shows that she cares about them and their work environment. Toward that end, here are some things you can do:

- Pick up trash in the parking lot.
- Listen to employees who complain that their cubicle or their office is too hot or too cold.

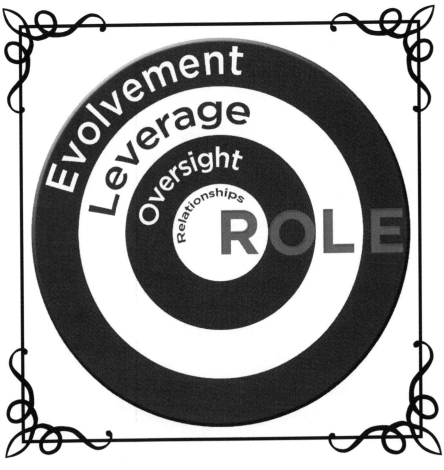

THE ROLE MODEL OF LEADERSHIP

- Allow them to turn their work space into a fun and friendly environment.
- Develop a corporate culture wherein workers have watchful care over the environment and each other.

In my current office, there was a dead roach on the floor in a little-used hallway. After the custodial staff ignored it for three days, someone took the time to create a sticky note and place it on the ground next to the dead roach. The words on the note read, "I am dead. Please throw me away!"

That roach stayed there for another couple of days before I saw it, whereby I promptly picked it up and threw it away. The situation was both funny and depressing at the same time. My teammates chose to leave the roach where it was, yet they let someone else (the custodial staff) know they weren't doing their job properly.

Leaders who have mastered the concept of oversight would have picked up the roach right away! They do not say, "It's not my job," "It's not my area," or any other non-involvement phrase. True leaders get involved and show oversight over their physical environments.

Leaders also need to improve themselves constantly – they need to Evolve. One of the biggest stumbling blocks to evolvement is a leader's current leader. At my job, I teach basic supervisory skills to city and county leaders. We spend time in classes, sharing ideas and best practices, but then the classes end. Although the knowledge and ideas they gain should influence their behavior back in the workplace, sometimes they do not. I send changed leaders back to their unchanged environments, and you can figure out what happens. Their leaders are stagnant and unwilling to change, and when these new, younger leaders attempt to evolve, they are reminded to keep their ideas to themselves and are told, "We've always done it this way."

Sometimes it feels like that statement is the rallying cry of poor-performing organizations. But it doesn't have to be that way. There are hundreds and hundreds of great leaders in civil service who want to evolve. They want to change themselves, they want to change their cultures; they want to become great leaders, and they want to leave legacies for the future. But they hit the roadblocks—their current leaders—and that's a hard speed bump to overcome.

Most high-performing employees constantly feel the need to evolve; they refuse to conform to the status quo. I began my career as a sportscaster. After two years I decided I wanted to work at Disney, and I started in attractions. I never planned on staying in one area too long. I transferred to become a resort front desk/ bell services host, then a front office manager, then an orientation consultant, then a college intern instructor, and then a leadership consultant, all because inside me I have this drive to evolve. That spirit still lives in me today.

The Disney theme parks are great examples of evolvement. When Walt was creating Disneyland, the most exciting part of it to him was that it would never be completed. It could hold all of his dreams. He marveled that even the trees would continue to grow. All Disney theme parks still evolve today. As attractions and entertainment options are replaced with others, they evolve and get better, and so do the employees.

One of the funny nuances of working for Disney is that one of the keys to success is to job-hop every two to three years. This shows that you are a versatile employee. I was a college intern instructor for about five years. I loved that role, but when I saw my peers out and about in the parks and resorts, the following dialogue would always occur:

"Hey, Pete, good to see you! Where are you working now?"

"I'm with the College Program as an instructor."

"Still?"

That always stuck with me—"Still?" The word always comes across when you stay in one job for too long. Part of the Disney culture is that if you're not up and moving around, you're getting stagnant. If you're in one location for two, three, or four years, people view you as having little motivation, though often that wasn't the case at all. People in that situation may just have found the perfect job for them.

This may exist in other organizations as well. I get the image of a stagnant pond with stuff floating on top, and I think of evolvement as a fountain in the middle of the pond. It's constantly moving the water, churning it, making the pond better, and that's what happens when we can evolve as leaders.

In addition to the oversight of your physical environment, you have to oversee your corporate culture. Just one person can have a tremendous influence on it. Corporate culture is often defined as "the way things are done around here."

Great leaders try and adjust their corporate culture in good times and bad. If sales are up, turnover is low, employees are getting along, and people enjoy coming to work, it's your job as a leader to feed that positive culture. Conversely, if you work in a challenging culture with backstabbing, gossip, and micromanaging, it's your job as a leader to influence that culture for the better. You need to be a positive influence, and you can only do that by staying connected to your culture via oversight.

JULIE WILLOZ ON A RARE COLD DAY IN FLORIDA

One way to influence the culture where you work is to lead by example. Julie Couret Willoz understood the importance of stepping in and working with the team when necessary:

> One of my fondest roles was as a guest service manager in Monorail Operations. My performance feedback indicated I was a well-respected leader, but the best feedback has come years later, as my former cast members in Monorails still tell me how much they enjoyed working for me. I believe it was the amount and quality of time I spent out in the operation, rain or shine.
>
> One story that stands out is when the Magic Kingdom Monorail Station was being renovated, and we had no station roof over two car lengths of train. The three o'clock parade had just ended, and we were experiencing another afternoon rainstorm. The line to board the Monorail was full and growing. We were not loading two cars of the train because not only would guests be standing in puddles and waiting in pounding rain, but so would our cast members who worked those gates. I could see the impact of the growing line with a nearly half-empty train on the cast and the guests.
>
> Even though I was dressed in my usual professional attire, I grabbed the floor squeegee and began to clear puddles from that area of the platform. Guests waited under the areas with roof coverage, and as a train came in I would go back out into the rain and load the guests myself. The wait time reduced significantly, and the guests were very grateful for my soaked-head-to-toe efforts.

It was my cast, however, who appreciated it the most. Because I demonstrated my willingness to get into the operation alongside them and put in the extra effort, we got much more than a faster load time. I earned their trust and respect. This created an even happier and more mutually satisfying work environment.

I learned that as leaders we cannot expect from our teams what we would not do ourselves. Whenever I was out in the operation, I could be found me loading trains, opening gates, and greeting guests. I would learn more from the cast members about their goals, their questions, and them as individuals through these experiences than I ever would have through structured one-on-ones.

— Julie Willoz

Julie is exactly right: great leaders know when to do office work and when to get out in the field with their employees. Most managers I knew had the exact same mindset as Julie no matter where they worked.

Another benefit of leading with oversight is that you move from a reactionary state to a preventive state. Disney Theme Parks are a great example. Before any new attraction opens, the company holds what they call a "test and adjust" period. During this time they work the ride, try new things, have soft openings, listen to feedback from the guests and the cast members, and then implement as many positive changes as they can before the attraction opens to the general public. This "test and adjust" concept applies not just to attractions but also to merchandise shops, food locations, and new entertainment venues. You can't have true oversight without open and honest feedback.

Back in the late 1980s, Universal Orlando (at the time it was Universal Studios Florida) and the Walt Disney World Resort were battling head to head to see which could open up their new movie studio theme park first. Along the way there was some lack of oversight by leadership at Universal Orlando, and their theme park opened with many challenges. Many of their biggest attractions was not operational on day one, and many guests left unhappy. The key lesson is that sometimes it's better to be right than to be first.

Disney is successful in training leaders because they communicate the minimum expectations. It's impossible for anyone in a leadership role at Disney to claim they don't know what it means to lead. For example, in the time that I worked at Disney, I had the following leadership guidelines to follow every day:

- The Disney Vision and Mission
- Disney Culture Statement
- Disney Values
- Disney Quality Standards
- Disney Traits and Behaviors
- Four Guest Expectations (from cast members)
- Four Cast Expectations (from their leaders)
- Performance Excellence Guidelines
- Our Purpose and Our Role
- Seven Guidelines for Guest Service

- Eight Cast Service Guidelines for Leaders of Leaders
- Seven Cast Service Guidelines for Front-Line Leaders
- Three Leadership Competencies
- Thirteen Great Leader Strategies

As a leader it was impossible to have all of these memorized. The great thing about some of these leadership strategies is that they applied to *all* cast members, which made it very easy to lead.

Lee Cockerell, former executive vice president of operations, rolled out a program called the Great Leader Strategies in the late '90s. The reason it was so well received was twofold: One, he modeled the strategies every day, and he invited all cast members to coach him if they ever saw him not following them. Two, he led training sessions on them approximately once a quarter.

Disney is a huge proponent of the "leaders as teachers" philosophy. No one is likely to follow thirteen leadership strategies that come from the human resources department packaged in posters and wallet cards. However, when the EVP of the entire resort shares the who, what, and why of these strategies, and invites *all* cast members to attend sessions to hear why they are important, it is much easier to get buy-in from all employees.

Lee also excelled by emulating two primary leadership strategies that are performed incorrectly in most organizations today: communication with all levels and approachability.

LEE COCKERELL, FORMER EVP OF WDW

Studies show that miscommunication is the number one cause of employee conflict in the workplace. When employees are in conflict, it carries over to the guest experience, which is never a good thing. Lee was passionate about making sure the correct message got to the cast members at the correct time. He wrote a weekly newsletter called "The Main Street Diary" where he shared leadership strategies, answered guest letters, and reminded cast members why we did what we did at Disney.

Perhaps no story better encompasses Lee's "lead by example" philosophy than the following. Below is an e-mail written by a high-ranking home-loan executive to his employees. In it he shares an encounter one of his family members had with Lee in August 2004.

The following is a **true story** and exhibits what can happen when the **right people build the right culture and believe** in [what] they are doing:

A week ago this past Sunday my daughter, son-in-law, and granddaughter were at the Orlando airport getting ready for a flight to Milwaukee, WI. They were traveling on a non-rev (airline employee) ticket. This meant they were subject to a dress code that included no tennis shoes, jeans, or shorts. This created a problem for my son-in-law, who had not packed any dress clothes for the vacation.

Attempting to find dress clothes at the Orlando airport on a Sunday evening proved futile. With a limited amount of time available, they called me while on the airport tram, explaining their dilemma to see if I could locate a department store near the airport via the Internet. Once off the phone I began the search, but did not hear back from the kids for an unusually long time. Finally they called back with enthusiasm in their voices that was quite the opposite of the previous phone call.

Catch this: A gentleman who was on that tram overheard the conversation. When the tram stopped, he offered my son-in-law his shoes and pants. They proceeded to a changing area, where the gentleman changed into another pair of pants he had with him, then gave my son-in-law his dress shoes and dress pants. This kind gentleman left the airport barefoot, giving my daughter his business card and suggesting they just forward the pants and shoes to his office after use.

To me this was and is an incredible act of kindness. **But for our purposes, it's something more.** All of us want to create a memorable experience for our clients and referral sources, but getting the culture **embedded into the very fabric of ourselves and our teams** is the real challenge. The act of this gentleman is more than him being kind — it is the very culture and fabric of the team at Disney. Turns out this gentleman is the executive vice president of operations at Disney. I think it is cool that the very top people in that culture live that culture EVERYWHERE they walk and live. *We* are the very top in our region, and I ask those around us at work, home, and play to say that we live the culture we strive for everywhere we walk and play. That is a conscious choice that we have the opportunity to make each morning. Best of success to all as we grow and get better at what we do!!!

Talk about leading by example!

Now, most Disney leaders don't have the chance to give up their pants. However, the little things are what get noticed:

- Picking up trash in the parks, or in the local shopping malls.
- Jumping in and helping when the guest lines are long.
- Showing respect and politeness at all times and in all situations.

While just reading about leadership in weekly newsletters may be helpful, nothing works better than good old-fashioned leadership development programs, and Disney is extremely good at this. During my time in Orlando, multiple leadership programs came and went via rebranding and organizational needs. They included the Disney Management Development Program (DMDP), the Disney Leadership Development Program (DLDP), CrossRoads to Leadership, and Emerging Leaders. While each program had to evolve to match the current needs, all had one thing in common: they were designed to impact leadership.

When I arrived at Disney in the '90s, their business model looked like this:

Cast Excellence – Guest Satisfaction – Business Results

The main component that was missing was leadership, as everything rises and falls on the leader. Therefore, the model changed to:

Leadership Excellence – Cast Excellence – Guest Satisfaction – Business Results

Another program Disney had in place to assist new leaders was called New Leader Transition. It was designed to help acclimate new leaders to their new culture. Since Disney is such a large organization, it's very common for leaders to move frequently for career growth and developmental opportunities. This could cause some issues with the front-line cast members, for just as they are creating relationships and bonding with their leader, upper management can come along and move the leader to a new area. While this is great for the leader, it can be a challenge for the cast members.

The New Leader Transition sessions were designed to lessen the startup time, prevent many of the early problems new managers create by over-managing or under-managing, and assist the current team members to understand the new leader's management style. While this process could not be applied to every person who transferred, it was used strategically and was (and continues to be) a successful way to transition leaders.

Another very successful way Disney walks the leadership walk is via their annual leadership conferences. With a cast member population of around fifty thousand, it's impossible to allow leaders to go out of town for continual training opportunities. The Disney University provides excellent internal training, but sometimes you can learn a lot more by getting out and around employees in other organizations to benchmark and share best practices.

The costs associated with this type of training would be enormous, so what did Disney do? They brought the leadership training to the cast.

In 2006 Walt Disney World began hosting its annual Leadership Conference. This two-day event was held in a convention center at one of the Disney resorts. Well-known keynote speakers were flown in from across the country to share their leadership messages; Vince Papale spoke on "Living your Dream," Alan Hobson talked of "The Triumph of Tenacity," Jim Kouzes inspired with "A Leader's Legacy," and more. Disney executives held roundtables, Disney legends shared their stories about Walt, and Disney trainers provided hundreds of workshop opportunities.

Having the conference over two days allows for coverage in the guest areas. The cost associated with putting on an annual conference of this type is enormous, yet Disney knows the return on investment they will receive from highly engaged leaders whose passion has been reignited.

Part of the problem with leadership today is that business and society have become okay with mediocrity — C's in schools are the new B's. I had a good friend in college who always said, "Dare to be average!" That's all anybody cares about, and I think some of this mentality may have taken over in business today.

Take a look at your neighborhood and any of the local businesses that have shut down recently. You can find any number of retail, food, or manufacturing locations that no longer exist. Some people blame it on the economy, and some blame it on bad luck, but at the end of the day most failures are the direct results of poor leadership. Leaders in those businesses did not make the right *relationships*, they didn't have the proper *oversight* of their business, they didn't *leverage* the right people, and in the end they failed to *evolve* (i.e. the ROLE Model). The reason those organizations did not reach their potential is they did not let their leaders reach *their* potential.

So what can we do about it? There are three main tasks I think current and future leaders need to address in order to use this ROLE model to help them reach their potential.

1. The first is for leaders to use the ROLE model to be a role model. In order to be a great leader you must first know thyself, as Socrates said. The ROLE model will do you no good if you don't know your values or what you stand for. That's the basis of

great leadership. Most leaders fail because they come across a troubling assignment and have to make a tough decision, and they don't have any internal basis for their decisions. You have to make sure you have a core set of values you will not shy away from no matter what it costs you.

2. Try to focus on one letter at a time instead of the whole model. If you're good at *relationships* (R), then go ahead and start with *oversight* (O). If you're good with both, then work on *leverage* (L). Just make sure you take the time to become successful at one instead of being so-so at all four.

   True leaders understand this process of becoming a great leader as ongoing — you will never come to a time when you've got it all. I'm not a perfect leader, you're not a perfect leader, and there are no perfect leaders out there who have conquered all four items in the ROLE method. That's because the last one, *evolvement* (E) means your journey will never be complete. You're always going to need to evolve as a leader to avoid failure.

3. Ask for help. I'm amazed by the number of people I have known over the years who were too proud to ask for assistance or feedback. We do not know everything, and there is nothing wrong with getting help. At Disney we were taught on the very first day, in our traditions orientation class, that when we put on the Disney nametag and walked

onstage in one of the parks or resorts, we were expected to know everything.

Now that wasn't true — we didn't know every-thing — but that is what the guests perceive: once you have a Disney nametag, you now know ev-erything! That's the image we wanted to project, but we knew it wasn't possible. So we set up many methods to assist the cast members to help them on their way towards knowing as much as they could about the organization — phone hotlines, a company intranet, open forums, meetings, etc.

All Disney cast members are trained never to say, "I don't know," but to say instead, "I don't know, but let's find out together." That puts the onus on the cast member to help the guest get the correct answer. At the same time, the cast member is self-developing his or her leadership skills. What a great model! As we're growing our potential, if we don't know something, let's find out together.

Putting it all together

As you can see, Disney does not have the magical secret to leadership. There is no magic formula. Success comes from leading by example, providing continual leadership training opportunities, and utilizing your successful leaders as teachers.

Now it's your turn! What can you do to improve your leadership skills? Use the worksheet on the next page to create three action items you can implement regarding leadership.

Action Items for Chapter Four: Enhancing Your Leadership Skills

List three things you can do to enhance your leadership skills:

#1

_____

_____

_____

_____

#2

_____

_____

_____

_____

#3

_____

_____

_____

FIVE
Chapter

Engage Them by Amplifying Your Recognition Methods

You can dream, create, design and build
the most wonderful place in the world...
but it requires people to make the dream a reality.

—Walt Disney

Recognition will always be linked to motivation, as mentioned back in chapter three. There are many ways to recognize employees. Some of you will look at these items and laugh, thinking there is no way any of them will work in your area. Remember we are purposefully keeping recognition and motivation together yet separate. All of these ideas are strictly ways to recognize your employees. They may or may not motivate them. But I can promise you this: there is very little chance they will de-motivate your staff, so why not give a couple of them a try?

Nametags

Disney is a first-name company. From the CEO to the newest cast members, everyone gets a nametag pin. They're a source of pride among the cast members. For years, the nametag consisted of Mickey Mouse on top with the cast member's name under him. They're a source of pride among the cast members. During special celebration years (the Millennium Celebration, the Year of a Million Dreams, the twenty-fifth anniversary), employees are issued new nametags with a different image other than Mickey Mouse on it. The cost of printing fifty thousand new nametags every few years is huge, but the Disney nametag has become synonymous with quality. They are constantly for sale on eBay and are considered collectors items.

Pins

Disney was a huge believer in pins. In fact one of my former managers at the Disney University had a pin board, which was nothing more than a bulletin board with all the pins on it. We frequently laughed at ourselves and said that work ethic would only get you so far — the reality was you were only as good as your pin board. The more pins you collected and were awarded, the longer your seniority and the more people you knew, the more you volunteered, and so on. There are many different types and styles of pins.

DISNEY NAMETAGS ARE WORN WITH PRIDE

CELEBRATION PINS

Celebration pins

These were given out frequently to wear for a limited time on your costume or work clothes. New attractions, movie openings, and even holidays brought out new celebration pins. True, they were also used for marketing purposes and to spark guest conversations, but it was amazing to see employees looking forward to them. In fact if you were sick on the day they were handed out, you were out of luck unless someone held one for you.

In your business you could make celebration pins and issue them for company anniversaries, limited edition merchandise, employee learning weeks, customer appreciation weeks, and so on.

Trainer pins

At Disney these have Jiminy Cricket on them—he who said, "Let your conscience be your guide"—along with the words "Disney Trainer." In order to be eligible for this pin, you must be recommended by your management team and then attend the Train the Trainer class offered through the Disney University. Without a proper trainer to onboard the new employees, retention and satisfaction rates of new employees may drop considerably. These pins are worn with pride by those who earn them.

Length-of-service pins

This topic can be very touchy depending on your corporate culture. At Disney, longevity is appreciated and rewarded. Pins that attach to your nametag are issued at one year and five years, and then in five-year increments after that. Each pin has a certain character associated with it and displays the number of years of service as well. From ten years on, they are offered in conjunction with a plaque or statue that matches the character on the pin.

Partners in Excellence pin and award

Also known as the PIE award, this is the most prestigious recognition a Disney Parks and Resorts cast member can achieve. It's peer-nominated and can only be issued after a highly in-depth process. This is *not* a "you nominate me and I'll nominate you" award, nor is it a "we have to give the employee of the month to someone, so let's give it to Tommy this time" award.

The PIE award is capped each year at the top three percent of each department. Each location can decide to give the award to fewer employees. Those who receive it are truly honored. It is based on cast excellence, guest satisfaction, and business results.

The award comes with a special pin the recipient can wear on his or her nametag, and a plated dinner with a famous guest speaker. It's a lifetime award, and recipients also gain special privileges, such as entrance to rides and attractions before they open to the rest of the cast and public.

Cast members will hold each other accountable and actively coach someone they see with a PIE pin who may not be performing as a PIE recipient should. Cast members who win this award are frequently looked at as mentors for other employees, and are frequently promoted as well.

LISA DOWNS IS A PROUD RECIPIENT OF THE
LEGACY NAMETAG AND PIN

The Walt Disney Legacy Award

The Walt Disney Legacy Award is a global program that recognizes the outstanding achievements of Walt Disney Parks and Resorts Cast, Crew and Imagineers who are selected by their leaders, direct reports and/or co-workers as top performers. These are individuals who consistently *Dream, Create* and *Inspire* each day by supporting the business objectives and goals of Walt Disney Parks and Resorts. This award came into being after I left the organization in 2007.

Perfect attendance awards

The basic idea was that cast members who did not use any sick time during a calendar year received a certificate and a cash award. While this was a good idea in principal, the unintentional side effect was that it encouraged cast members to come to work sick, thus affecting their coworkers who also refused to call in sick in an attempt to gain the yearly bonus. The end result was lots of coughing and hacking. This award was discontinued in the late 1990s.

Quarterly awards

These were resort and theme park specific, and were presented as a type of "employee of the quarter" award. Similar to the PIE award, these did *not* have a minimum expected number of recipients. If there was no one eligible for it in a department, then that department did not have a representative.

The award came with a certificate and usually included some type of get-together with the highest-ranking manager. For example winners at Port Orleans Resort would receive a lunch with the general manager of the hotel in one of the hotel restaurants.

Thank-you notes

Never ever underestimate the power of a handwritten thank-you note. This concept was ingrained into me from day one as a Disney leader. With all the technology available today, it is so easy to send a thank-you text or e-mail. While I do not want to minimize those channels of distribution (after all, anything is better than nothing), the handwritten note will still take you farther than you would expect.

I give thank-you notes out in my current job. Some employees have let me know they have worked there for more than ten years and never received one. Brian, one of my coworkers at Disney University, received one from a vice president of employee relations. He had it mounted on a plaque and hung it over his desk. I have seen other employees frame them and hang them up as well.

The higher up the note comes from, the more weight it carries. If you are a CEO, president, or high-ranking official and you make time to send a thank-you note to

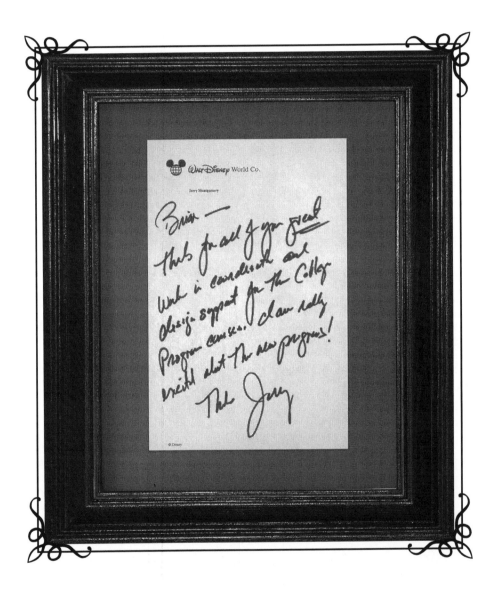

THE POWER OF A THANK YOU NOTE

a front-line employee, it may have a longer benefit to that person than any 1 percent raise or $250 bonus. The handwritten note may take a little more time than an e-mail, but the rewards far outweigh the costs.

Donuts

I know this sounds crazy, but food can and should be used as a recognition tool. The problem happens when the donuts go from a means of recognition to symbols of entitlement. We've all been there—you want to thank your team for working hard, and you stop on the way in to work and bring in two dozen Krispy Kremes for the staff meeting. Everyone is very appreciative. Fast forward to next week's staff meeting, and what is the first thing you hear? "Where are the donuts?"

The donuts are now an *expectation* at every meeting. But not to worry—this can be fixed simply by treating your employees like third graders. The next time you want to use food as a recognition tool, the following speech must accompany it:

> "Good morning, everyone. I brought in donuts today. They are my way of saying 'thank you' for all your hard work on the Vagi project. You all put in many hours this past week, and I want to let you know your hard work has not gone unnoticed. These donuts are just a small token of appreciation.
>
> Please keep in mind that these donuts are to thank you for your work on the Vagi project and should not

be expected at every staff meeting. Otherwise they would lose their specialness. Thanks again for all you did this week—now let's dig in."

As corny as that sounds, it works. If you don't believe me, just bring food to your next meeting and don't speak those words, and watch what happens at the next event.

A recognition budget

Some employers get it, and some don't. Those who don't will look at this idea and think I'm crazy.

When I was at Disney, I had a line item in my budget for recognition. It wasn't much, but it was there. It allowed me to do nice things for my employees when I needed to. Perhaps I would take someone to lunch. Maybe I would send someone to an off-property training session. Movie tickets and miniature golf vouchers went a long way.

This has become a lot easier with the advent of gift cards. It used to be you had to drive to the restaurant to buy a gift certificate. Now all you have to do is go down to you local grocery store or pharmacy and stock up on $10 restaurant cards, entertainment cards, and even generic Visa cards.

The next time you have to prepare your annual budget, put a little extra in there for employee recognition. You will be glad you did, and so will your employees.

Training classes

As a trainer, I might be a little biased here, but I have always viewed training as a form of recognition. Unfortunately, many organizations and departments use it as punishment: "You messed up, so you need to go to customer service/workplace harassment/diversity training."

I see training and development as one and the same. Training classes can and should be used for employees who are lifelong learners. Many of your employees would probably be very excited to attend a training program or one-day conference that is not held in their workplace. Yes, they get out of the office for the day, but it's much more than that. It gives them a sense of pride and a sense of accomplishment and lets them know that they are appreciated.

You could even take it to the next level and have the employees create a lunch-and-learn session when they return, to share what they learned and what they will apply. Don't ever underestimate the power of learning.

Tuition reimbursement

This may not be a form of recognition per se, but it is still a perk many employees do not take advantage of. Disney had a very thorough policy that allowed employees to take classes at many local universities. The cost of tuition *and* books would be reimbursed as long as the class was directly related to the job the employee was currently performing. This prevented someone in accounting from going back to school to get a law degree on Disney's dime.

If your company currently has a tuition reimbursement policy, it's time for you to take a good, hard look at it and make sure it's being used properly. A policy that is unfriendly and cumbersome to employees can be worse than no policy at all.

Outings and team days

Most offices are drab, dull, cubicle-driven environments with long halls and echo-filled conference rooms. Why are you and your team not getting out of the office at least once a year, if not more often? Any chance to get out into some new surroundings *is sure* to stimulate creativity and innovation.

Disney is the exception to this rule. Just about every backstage area has some type of color, theme, or character to it. The Disney University is one of the most colorful and themed buildings I have ever worked in. It makes sense, as it's the second place of the company most new hires see (the first is the casting building, where they are hired).

As you approach the DU for your first day of work, the doors slide open and your senses are immediately stimulated. You can smell fresh coffee from the employee cafeteria, aptly named the Stage Door. A Mickey Mouse statue and comfortable, colorful couches beckon you to enter farther. Four televisions on the wall are tuned to Disney information channels for both the guests and the cast members. A look up to the ceiling shows a blue sky with lots of clouds—but upon closer look, you can make out some Disney characters in the clouds.

As you move down a hallway to a classroom for your first day of orientation, a multimedia timeline along the wall shares the histories of the company and of Walt Disney himself. With a building like this, why would you need to go somewhere else to stimulate creativity and innovation?

At Walt Disney World, all employees must attend their orientation program at the Disney University. This training session is known as Disney Traditions. This interactive training program runs between one and two days and includes instructor-led training, role plays, videos, and a trip to the Magic Kingdom to experience the magic in action.

One of my peers at Disney had a special way of recognizing employees on their *first* day of work!

RUSS ROTHAMER (FAR LEFT) AND HIS GOOFY TEAM

Russ Rothamer is now the Vice President of Academic Affairs at Coconino Community College in Flagstaff, Arizona. I worked with him when he was the manager of segment learning and development for The Walt Disney Company. Here is his story:

> I had a friend, Jill, who I had met through our Executive MBA Program at the University of Florida. She worked in marketing for years at Publix, a large grocery chain. She had a dream to work for Disney. Her dream became a reality. I also was fortunate enough to work at Disney University with the College Education Team.
>
> A cast member's first day at Disney is special, as you get to attend Traditions. I wanted to make Jill's day even more special. At that time, character training was taking place in Disney University, and I worked it out with the leader so Chip and Dale would pay Jill a visit in her Traditions class. They presented her with a Magical Moments card and a Mickey Mouse plush. She was so excited she cried.
>
> She called me later that night to thank me and cried all over again. She said it was the best day of work ever. From the learning and development side, the Traditions facilitators were able to use this magical moment as an example of the opportunities cast members have to make special, memorable moments for guests and their fellow cast members.
>
> — *Russ Rothamer*

When you work somewhere long enough—and that includes Disney—a building becomes just that: a building. We would often book conference rooms at other

Disney hotels. Epcot contained many hidden confer-ence rooms in the pavilions; some cast members didn't even know they existed. What great places to have a brainstorming meeting.

If you don't work at Walt Disney World and don't have access to such facilities, where can you go? How about a conference room at an outdoor store? Gander Mtn. and Bass Pro Shops both have conference rooms attached to their gigantic stores. You could allow your employees to wander the stores before and after your meeting.

How about local places of interest? City museums and historical sites often have meeting places that are available to organizations. If they're too expensive to book for a full day, see if you can barter. Perhaps you can provide the venue with some advertising or train-ing opportunities with your company.

The bottom line is just to get away. And remember, when you do, you need to remind your employees this is a form of recognition. You could be meeting in the same old boring conference room, but you want to get out for half a day to thank them for all they've been do-ing. Trust me — most employees will like the idea.

Guest service cards

In the thirteen years I worked at Disney, I came across many different recognition programs. Some were local and some were company-wide. One program that has stood the test of time is called the Guest Service Fanatic (GSF) card (later changed to *Great* Service Fanatic).

Managers cannot be everywhere at once. In fact, most of the time, a manager may not even know all the good things that happen in his own area. The GSF program is, for the most part, a peer-recognition program. It's very simplistic in its approach. When a cast member sees a fellow cast member going above and beyond for a guest or a fellow employee, she can fill out a GSF card with the person's name, the date, and the story of what she witnessed. She can then present the card to the cast member to let him know she saw him going above and beyond.

At that point, the CM (Cast Member) who received the card places it into the GSF box in his area. This is not an old shoebox with some wrapping paper on it. The GSF boxes are well-made, heavily branded, and have locks on them. Once a month the HR manager or a designee takes all the cards out of the box and does three things with them.

First, the card is placed into the employee's permanent file. Then, there's a drawing for prizes for that month. Finally, the card is hole-punched to notify the CM it was in the box and has been noted, and it is sent back to the CM for him to keep.

You would be surprised how many CMs kept all of their cards in scrapbooks or posted them on their work cubes. Some even had them framed. The reason is it was a *company-wide* initiative. Everyone from the CEO down knew and participated in this program.

In addition, any cast member who was a guest in the park on his days off could fill out a GSF card and issue it. Wow. What a surprise for a CM who thinks no one is watching her. That's when it's fun to go to work.

Putting it all together

Now it's your turn! What can you do to keep your employees engaged? Use the worksheet on the next page to create three action items you can implement regarding recognition.

Action Items for Chapter Five: Amplifying Your Recognition Methods

List three things you can do to recognize your employees:

#1

#2

#3

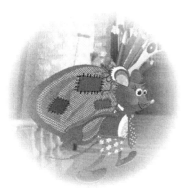

SIX
CHAPTER

ENGAGE THEM WITH PARTNERING AND RELATIONSHIP BUILDING

Every man is captain of his career
and there must be cooperation all around if he is to
get what he wants out of life.

—Walt Disney

Thirty thousand acres. Forty-seven square miles. More than fifty thousand employees. And that's just the Walt Disney World Resort in Orlando.

My biggest fear when I started working with Disney was getting lost in the shuffle. (Granted, when I began my career in 1994, there were only thirty thousand cast members — but that didn't make it any easier!)

I knew I wanted to make Disney my career, yet I had no idea how to work my way up. The basic skill that I learned early on, and that I used on a daily basis, dealt with networking and building relationships. If there was ever a company that believes it's not what you know, it's who you know, it's Disney!

Relationships are how work gets done. When you're dealing with as many employees and as large a property as we had at Disney, it's essential to know as many people as you can. That's why the first key to making a large company feel small is building relationships.

Creating relationships is not easy for everyone. Some people don't want to take the time to develop them; some may not have the personality to pull it off; some people may just be jerks — and therefore no one wants to have a relationship with them!

Keep in mind that I'm not talking about favoritism, or brown-nosing, or kissing up to the boss, or any other negative action. I am speaking strictly from personal experience which has shown me the more people you know, the more you can do, and the faster it can get done.

Each year, WDW would host approximately eight thousand interns in the Walt Disney World College Program. One of my projects at the Disney University was to create an experiential learning component for the college program interns that would immerse them into the forty-seven square miles of WDW that we affectionately called the world's largest learning laboratory.

I originally thought to call it the Disney Enlightenment Series. The cast members who would lead these sessions would then be known as the Disney Enlightenmentors — or the Enlighten-mentors. Either way, I thought, it was a big win. However, the name did not pass muster, and therefore the project became known simply as the Disney Exploration Series.

My goal was to create a series of classes, tours, etc. based on topics such as communication, hospitality, and human resources. This project, though big in scope, was a breeze to complete because of my relationships. Getting others onboard was just a phone call or an e-mail away.

Another key to making a big company feel small is to make sure the employees know they are making a difference and everything they do matters. If you work at Epcot, you have no control over what happens at the Magic Kingdom. If you work in food and beverage, you have no control over what happens in attractions. What you *can* control is your department, your shift, or your precinct.

Understanding what you can control was often explained via the concept of "big picture to small parts". For example cast members who worked in the kitchens of quick-service restaurants were not just cooking burgers. They believed a family was going to come to *their* theme park and *their* restaurant, and that family was going to order four of *their* cheeseburgers, and that family was going to enjoy that meal as a part of their Disney vacation. Training every cast member to know how important *their* role was to the entire show created more-committed employees.

About a year before I left the Disney company, many departments were creating what was known as a *segment reorganization*. The Walt Disney Company was the segment, and the locations were known as *sites*. I was a member of the Career and Professional Development Team segment. My sites were my partners at Walt Disney World, Disneyland, Disney Cruise Line, and Walt Disney Imagineering. You can imagine how important it was during this transition to have relationships, and to think of the business from big picture to small parts.

The third and final way to make a big company feel small is to have the right leaders in place. It's imperative that leaders not forget where they came from. When a leader becomes too big for his or her britches, employees can feel half a world away. Great leaders connect with their employees and get them to understand the importance of their roles—no matter how big or how small.

Relationships are not just about one-on-one connections. In business, you need to make sure people in certain departments have good working relationships with each other. An example would be public safety, where people in the dispatch department had better have good relationships with the officers. Do the people in your accounting department have a good relationship with those in your operations department? You never know when they're going to need each other.

I was a front office manager at Disney's Port Orleans Resort for a couple of years. The front desk staff needed to have good relationships with the housekeeping staff. Check-in time was always three o'clock in the afternoon. To our guests this meant their rooms would be ready at three o'clock and not one second later. When rooms were not cleaned by three o'clock, some cast members' first reactions were to find out who was to blame:

> "I told housekeeping these people need their room at three o'clock."

> "What could they possibly be doing down there? They had all day to clean this room!"

> "I'm sorry, sir, but our housekeeping staff must be behind schedule today."

Playing the blame game doesn't do anything to help build relationships. The best thing for us to do in that case was to figure out how to solve the main issue, which was that rooms were not clean at three o'clock. We made sure all of our front desk managers and house-keeping managers were cross-utilized, shadowed each other's departments, and did shifts in each other's de-partments. Once you work in a housekeeping location for a week, you come back with a whole different idea of why some rooms may not be ready at three o'clock.

BART LEAHY (BACK LEFT) WITH HIS FRIENDS AT
A SERVICE CELEBRATION EVENT

One of my peers at the front desk was Bart Leahy, who is now a senior technical writer for the NASA Marshall Space Flight Center. In addition to the front desk, he worked in a department called Guest Letters. Back in the 1990s, with no Internet or e-mail, letters were our primary way to communicate with our guests. Bart had many interesting experiences when responding to guest letters, and one directly related to partnering and relationships:

> When I worked in the Guest Letters department, I quickly gained a reputation for my willingness to answer the unusual letters. These could range from uncommon requests to questions about Disney trivia, and often required calling multiple parks, resorts, or departments to answer.
>
> The trick, I quickly learned, wasn't to know everything but to know whom to call. One source of information I could always count on was MK-07 (Magic Kingdom Operations). Once a concerned parent asked me where he could find manually flushing toilets because his child was afraid of the automatic flushers. The MK-07 hostess giggled but got back to me with the information.
>
> A few weeks later, a woman wrote asking if there was still a Dumbo with a purple hat on a particular attraction. She wanted to know because her daughter had died recently and the last picture she had of them together was on that Dumbo; she wanted to ride it again.
>
> When I called MK-07 and asked my question, the response was, "Is this the guy who wanted to know about the automatically flushing toilets?" I admitted

it was, and the cast member and I had a good laugh about that. But again she made the appropriate calls and got back to me with the answer (yes, the purple-hatted Dumbo was still there).

I think MK-07 had a lot of fun with my phone calls, but they always knew I was serious about my questions, and I always knew I could count on them (or any other department), as the experts, to get the answers right.

— Bart Leahy

Relationships are less about the blame game and more about how to get people in your departments to work together.

The concept of relationships can take a turn for the worse if people try to use them to gain backdoor access or to circumvent the system. However, if done properly, they can add another valuable resource for you as a leader (especially if you build them across multiple layers).

We get so bogged down in the business world today, separating ourselves by titles and levels and what our company IDs say we are — hourly or salaried, exempt or nonexempt, and so on. The first thing you need to do is break down barriers and establish yourself as a leader who is going to work with anyone and everyone.

Amy Kesman Rossi also worked at Epcot and, through partnerships, she was able to assist her cast members both professionally and financially:

We had about forty College Program participants in the cast of Tapestry of Nations at Epcot, but the parade shift was only four hours long. I partnered with the labor team at Epcot to find other locations that would be willing to have these students work with them for four hours before their Tapestry shifts. Food & Beverage and Custodial were the primary partners.

This was a tremendous success all around. These areas gained extra help during a busy time of day, we were able to provide CP students with the unique opportunity of performing in our parade, and the students gained work experience in two areas instead of just one.

– Amy Kesman Rossi

Amy could have sat back and told these cast members they had four-hour shifts and that was all they could have. But by using her connections and having a passion for her team, she was able to provide for both her cast and the company's bottom line.

Social networking is very popular these days, and the current rage is to gain as many contacts or friends as you can on your Facebook, LinkedIn, or Twitter account. You may have two thousand friends online, but only two hundred of those are based on quality relationships. The other eighteen hundred are not really relationships, which are based on time, attitudes, feelings, and behaviors. Nobody wants to have a relationship with someone who isn't putting in the time and effort.

Today, relationships are global! They are built via computers and the Internet. The web allows us to build relationships all around the world. As a business professional and current leader, you need to be web 2.0 savvy. You need accounts on LinkedIn, Facebook, and Twitter. You need to have an electronic presence, as relationships are being built in a whole different realm than they used to be. There will always be power lunches, coffee breaks, and water-cooler talk, but if you do not have an electronic presence in the world of relationship building, you are going to fall behind.

Using leverage to your advantage

In chapter four, the concept of *Leverage* was introduced as part of the ROLE model of leadership. Relationships are built though *leverage*—a concept as simple as a see-saw. Have you ever seen anyone having fun on a see-saw alone? Probably not. The person just sits there until someone else comes along, and that is when the fun starts. A great definition of leverage is the power or ability to influence people, events, and decisions.

Let's begin with the very first word in this definition: power. Most people know there are many different types of power—position, referent, legitimate, and so on. While power can be used in a positive way, it can also corrupt. Similarly, leverage is where most leaders can get tripped up. To return to the see-saw example, when one person jumps off at the top, the other person is left to crash down, bottom first, onto the ground.

That's a harmful use of leverage. When it's used incorrectly, it can cause undue harm to a leader. People sometimes use leverage for their own personal gain. They use others and give nothing back in return. This tactic can weaken your personal brand and leave you stranded when you need assistance as a leader.

There are multiple ways to apply leverage in an organization. But be careful! Look at big, private companies like Enron and smaller government agencies across the United States, and you'll find someone in leadership is using leverage in a way he or she shouldn't be. Beware of the power of leverage.

True leaders will use influence to gain the leverage they need. So many leaders, even today, still rely on what I call the old demand and command model of leadership instead of the influence and inspire model that's needed today.

Back in the 1950s, Walt Disney was trying to get funding to build Disneyland, which was going to be the first ever theme park. He wanted to build it in California. Getting that much funding back in those days was not an easy task, especially for such an unknown venture.

Walt got in touch with the ABC television network, and they actually used each other as leverage. Disney needed funding; ABC was a distant third in the ratings and needed some top-notch programming. In a metaphorical sense, both of them were sitting on their seesaws alone. They were not having any fun until they got together, and that was when success started to happen.

What happened with Disneyland and ABC could also be termed *partnering*, which is a huge part of leverage. In the business world, success comes with having multiple partners who will work with you because you can't do it alone.

Putting it all together

Now it's your turn! What can you do to build your partnerships and relationships? Use the worksheet on the next page to create three action items that you can implement regarding partnering and relationship building.

Action Items for Chapter Six: Partnering and Building Relationships

List three things you can do to partner or build relationships:

#1

#2

#3

Conclusion

Employee Engagement is not a flavor of the month nor is it a leadership gimmick. It is a measureable trait that explains the pulse of your company or organization.

It is my hope that these thoughts have given you at a few ideas that you can try to implement in your organization.

Remember, engagement goes up when you focus on your employees first and customers second. It works for companies like Southwest Airlines, Ritz-Carlton and Disney. Why shouldn't it work for you?

Thanks for reading, and I wish you the best. Go engage those employees!

Book **Pete Blank** for your next speaking engagement!

The principles, ideas, and strategies that Pete shares in this book are incorporated into his speeches and seminars that he conducts across the United States. Listed below are some of his most popular sessions.

Put a Little Disney Magic in your Organization

Disney is not the only company that provides magic. Your organization needs to provide memorable and magical experiences for both your customers and your employees. This session focuses on how the Disney organization makes magic with setting, branding, process improvement, employee loyalty, teamwork and more. You will learn easy ways on how YOU can implement some Disney MAGIC into your organization!

The Disney Way of Customer Service

If you have ever visited a Disney Theme Park across the globe, you may feel that "nobody does customer service like Disney". Although the execution is complex, the baseline concepts are quite simple. In this session, you will uncover some basic customer service strategies from Walt Disney himself. You will then learn how to apply these lessons in your own organization in an effort to enhance the customer service in your department.

Enhancing your Leadership Skills the Disney Way

Leaders are made and not born. Today's leaders are being asked to be managers, counselors, trusted advisors and technical experts. But leaders cannot lead others unless they are confident in their own leadership style. In this fun and interactive session, we will...

- Discover how successful organizations (such as Disney) train their leaders

- Learn the four characteristics of the ROLE Model of Leadership

- Understand how Disney positions its leadership team to add organizational value

Employee Engagement: Lessons from the Mouse House

Based on the book by the same name, Pete shares six ways to maximize your employee's engagement levels.

For more information, please visit Pete's website at www.peteblank.com, or you can contact him at:

peteblank@peteblank.com
407-376-8384

Made in the
USA
Middletown, DE

77356502R00080